UNHEARD MELODIES

Robert MacIsaac

Unheard Melodies

EVERY BOOK PRESS
OREGON HOUSE
MMX

Contents

"Heard melodies are sweet, but those unheard
Are sweeter..."

John Keats

for Solee

A Song for Spring

Sing a song of perfume winds!
Sing a song of peeping seeds!
Sing as blossoms float their pins
And maidens pluck the choking weeds.
Laugh and cry!
Jump so high!
All through the rosy day.
Dance and sing!
All sorrows fling!
For winter's far away.

Sing a song of bleating sheep!
Sing a song of thistle down!
Sing as Nature teases sleep
With shaking dewdrops off her gown.
My heels click
Like eyelids quick,
And scamper through the grass;
My chilly feet,
The flowers sweet
And loves that never pass.

Sing a song of laughing girls!
Sing a song of daffodils!
Sing as Pan with reedy skirls
Delights the wood nymphs on the hills.
The cloudlets burst
To sate our thirst
And water everyone;
And with a sigh
The angels spry
Dash foaming to the sun.

🕊 *Ballad*

Thousands and thousands of pennies have I,
And a bottle of brandy too;
Yet I'd cast them away for a violet eye
That looks tenderly
At me.

Hundreds and hundreds of wishes have I,
And a chatterbox for a brain;
But I'd toss them aside for one sweetened reply
That speaks dear
Zu mir.

Dozens and dozens of secrets have I,
And a clandestine friend within;
Still I'd offer him up for just pie in the sky,
With a song in my throat and a wink in my eye,
And never would stop to ask myself why,
If we'd be
You and me.

A Wedding Song

Once on a fragrant, breezy day
Sir Cupid buzzed around a tree;
He picked and tossed some leaves away,
Then laughing, perched and said to me:
"I see your gloomy eyelids stare
"And calculate another sigh;
"You should pretend you're standing bare
"And spread your arms out to the sky!"
"Oh no, Sir Eros, you are wrong,
"I try so hard to love my friend.
"I think about it all day long
"Until I know what I should send."
"This is not love!" "How so?" "It's not!
"You're madder than Apollo's niece!"
"I try..." "You lose!" "...I ne'er forgot
"What I should say..." "My good man, cease!"
"But love is very personal:
"I have, I give, I take, I kiss.
"I do my work." "I curse it all!"
"But you?..." "That's right! I conjure this!
"But this," he paused and cocked his head
Up to the blue and brilliant sky,
"Up there is love! Not in your bed,
"Nor in your rose or nose or eye!"
"It's where?" "Up there!" "I do not see."
"Then burst your wings and catch the wind!
"Arise, and fly up after me!"
"I..." "Up!" We soared! I gasped and grinned.
We hurtled through the giddy air
And stroked and kissed a thousand maids;
We bounced and twirled without a care,
Then sank and panted in these shades.
I still stand here beneath this bough
And watch the light caress each limb,
Sometimes, my Love, I see you now;
Sometimes I love you, just like Him.

Open Door

One day amid the woods I spied
A house beneath a spreading tree;
Some said its door would open wide,
If only we could find the key.
I asked, but everyone denied
And said, "We must wait patiently.
"There's lots of time – please, have some tea."

Seizing an axe I cried, "What for?
"It's clear enough we've naught to lose!"
My windmill hands besieged the door,
Then brushed the splinters off my shoes.
I entered and saw hallways four
With many stairs and rooms – how choose?
I shrugged, and settled for a snooze.

But then a laugh disturbed my dream,
And then a whisper burned my ear;
I woke and saw a merry gleam
Dance far away and hover near;
Its two pinpoints of light did seem
To note my every smile and fear –
I saw them wink, then disappear.

I rushed into the paneled hall
And saw her foot trip up the stair.
With anxious words I tried to call
And begged her just to linger there;
One moment did she seem to stall –
I flew up as if through the air.
She started laughing, everywhere.

At first I seemed to hold her fast,
But then she called from far away;
That way I went, but then she passed
And settled save where I would stay.

Throughout this labyrinth I dashed
Declaiming, "I just want to play!"
She cried, "Then clean the house today!"

Begrudgingly I snatched a broom
And washed and swept till I was numb;
I cleaned and painted every room
With tired arm and swollen thumb.
I could have seen her shadow loom
Or heard her sweet, melodious hum,
But I forgot that she might come;

So I resolved to give it up,
And turned, But oh! Her hair did shine!
She handed me a diamond cup
Glowing full of amber wine.
On fruits and dainties we made sup,
And she discoursed in words divine:
I was no more, and she was mine.

Again I stand before this door
And bang at it with feeble will;
Sometimes it seems we can't do more,
Sometimes it seems we've had our fill.
And yet perhaps she sees our chore
And calls to us with happy trill,
Beckoning from – the windowsill!

Ballad for Insomnia

I met an old man, and the man did speak,
With a heigh and a ho and the world don't know,
He asked me where was the end of last week,
And the world won't go if the winds don't blow.

His warring eyes were red but keen,
With a heigh and a ho and the world don't know,
And flared the loss of wisdom's sheen,
And the world won't go if the winds don't blow.

I told him that I was a young lad,
With a heigh and a ho and the world don't know,
He said, "Innocence ain't cause to be sad,"
And the world won't go if the winds don't blow.

I pointed to my raggéd feet,
With a heigh and a ho and the world don't know,
He said that vanity lives in the street,
And the world won't go if the winds don't blow.

I asked, "Kind sir, can you tell me why,"
With a heigh and a ho and the world don't know,
"A passing cloud can make you cry?"
And the world won't go if the winds don't blow.

He looked at me and started to laugh,
With a heigh and a ho and the world don't know,
"Jesus said they'd fling out the chaff,"
And the world won't go if the winds don't blow.

"The world is melting, little friend,"
With a heigh and a ho and the world don't know,
"And a beating heart don't beat the end,"
And the world won't go if the winds don't blow.

The grey sky growled, the dry leaves wept,
With a heigh and a ho and the world don't know,
And like the dead my burdens slept,
And the world won't go if the winds don't blow.

I bowed and said, "I'm off to bed,"
With a heigh and a ho and the world don't know,
He cried, "Why don't it rain instead!"
And the world won't go if the winds don't blow.

But ever since the storms they roar,
With a heigh and a ho and the world don't know,
And beat against my bedroom door,
And the world won't go if the winds don't blow.

There is abandon in the dawn,
There is abandon in the night;
Abandon when our sorrows spawn,
Abandon when the hour is right,
And even when
There is no light.

There is abandon with a kiss,
There is abandon with a friend;
Abandon when our yearnings miss,
Abandon when our love we send
And know that it
Will not pretend.

There is abandon in a crowd,
There is abandon on a stair;
Abandon when our world is loud,
Abandon when we want to care,
But want this only
In despair.

There is abandon of the heart,
There is abandon of a deed;
Abandon when our eyelids part,
Abandon when they start to plead
And know not this
Is what we need.

There is abandon of a dream,
There is abandon of a hate;
Abandon when desires teem,
Abandon when our hands create
And show to us
Our own portrait.

Let me abandon when I speak,
Let me abandon when I do;
To find that everything I seek
Is nothing less than seeking you,
I will not lack
For what is true.

There is a charm in letting go,
There is a wish to open wide;
If I abandon what I know,
I know I still need never hide,
Even when darkness
Sleeps by my side.

Something fluttered before my face –
I brushed it off and tried to dream.
It came again and teased my brow:
My quick hand flicked the air alone.
Once more this nagging pest returned,
And I would snatch and crush its wing,
If only it would linger here
And let me watch its drubbing fans.
Instead, it whizzes when I stare
And start to raise my open palm;
It hums around my sleeping ear;
It calls me names in grey twilight.
To capture it I sewed a net,
Which I wear loosely round my neck
And fondle as I lightly doze.
Now it giggles above my head,
Now it chides me to ungird,
It trips behind me as I walk,
And when I speak, it echoes me.
Yet even when it goes away
And lets me rest for several days,
I walk, and watch, and cannot sleep
And drag my net along the ground.

🪶 *Leonardo's Cartoon*

Are you aware of this? Why be so kind?
You may be thoughtful, sweet, yet never find.
He struggles at your breast – don't let Him go.
You rest on me; you need me, and I know,
I know what you should do. (Look where it points!
Look!) Are you aware? For you almost smiled.
That gentle face, so like her gentle Child.
Her purpose is to see Him, His to bless
And reach toward another tenderness,
The yielding glance of understanding death.
So softly do we take the precious breath,
As their soft robes receive the dawning light;
And our feet would rest, but then the flight
That's in this, too

Ars Amoris

Lotus petals fall from Gautama's eyes,
His lap receives them, his smile never dies;
Jacob wrestled an angel to the earth,
That desert gave a suffering people birth.

Where men of Hellas cut the ivory stone
Athena gazes from a raggéd throne;
The Nazarene drew wisdom in the dust,
On water we follow, His blood we trust.

What I say to you I say to no one else.
This only time accepts these furtive words
That we impart but once. E'en though I love
Another, and though another meeting
Discloses only tea and mild politesse,
I say to you what was not said before.
Who chose the hour, when secrets tempted love,
And yearnings of our soul and mind enchant
A quiet walk? Who knows what other breast
May guard our weariness, what other voice,
Awash with our sigh, may whisper understandings
Only distance can descry? A god o'erleaps
A million worlds. We rise, and turn before
Each other, clustered stars agape with light
That eye to eye unsettle lonely night.

✆ *The Charioteer at Delphi*

Stillness. Behind every word we utter,
Behind every grimace, smile, uncertain frown,
Flexing and unflexing of hate or love,
Stands our silent pillar of existence.
And so standest thou, a slender bronze taper,
Whose glowing eyes burn with steady watchfulness.
Art thou guiding, or merely pulled along
In regal submission by thy flowing
Phantom train? But no. The awesome heavens
Neither lead nor trail this world's celestial
Statement; they speak the unutterable will
Of light eternal, and gaze abeyant
Over and through our own impulsive stance.
And so seést thou, and wait; wait for us
To part the mottled veil of strict emphasis,
Unloose ourselves from what we disregard
And touch with clearing eyes the dearer heart,
As firmly as thy shining feet inform
The earth. And rooted thus – still, open, true –
May we rise a solid presence, and with
Our own prancing team, fly on fervent wings
To greet and honor the prophetic sun.

𝔄 At Afaia

O! thou must sigh thy love unto the East,
And suffer not this moment to display;
Charming words describe, but cannot say
How hope endured and doubt forever ceased.
When silken maids ascended to the feast
In Hera's marble hall, the prophet's lay
Unfurled in anguish; but with reverence they
Disposed Her dreaded hour. And love increased.
And love undid their flowing hair, and love
Prepared the calf; and with his rising bliss
Perfumed incense curled columns to the sky,
Their fevered chant implored the powers high,
And one by one their tears each other kissed
And stroked his brow that thundered from above.

The Parthenon Frieze

Take me to Athens, let me walk with them:
Let nimble youths run by with sheep and goats;
Let merchants offer figs beside the road,
And rascals try to throw them Persian coins;
Let women pass with beads and plaited tress
And urns of oil on shoulder or on hip;
Let riders stiffly jostle on their steeds,
With swords and shields clacking on their backs;
Let friendly shoulders bear a friendly arm
As each to each the bearded elders speak;
Let mothers give their children leaves of palm,
Who wave them happily in each others' faces;
Let girls with flutes and tambours softly amble
And mingle pipe and timpani with chatter;
Let lovers walk apart and watch each other;
Let soldiers tie the leather round their swords;
Let herdsmen strike the bulls and shout behind them;
Let poets bear the scrolls and waxen tables;
Let statesmen be the first to reach the summit –
Beneath them songs and lowing in the sun,
A line of dust, with robed and naked figures
Tanned and glistened with athletic joy,
Each fold and sinew replete with new ecstasy; –
And so they turn, and mount the final step,
Passing through porticoes flanked by cool columns,
Rose and burnished gildings mute with dim shades,
Chiseled figures aglow by teasing fires
Curling lithely in their brazen sockets;
Hints of incense seep through tenantless chambers,
A chair unused, a dais without prophet,
Hallowed emptiness rising to enshroud
Blessed rites and song no longer needed;
They never speak, but, furtive with their gaze,
Their breath awash with awe, admire silence:
No idle look, no flush, no aimless cackle,
No sidelong trespass flails before their eyes;
Cleaned by hard light and fragrant wisps of air,

They, affright with greeting a love they dread,
Behold, now back enow bestrewn with grace,
Impossible gods impossibly at ease,
Each limb and visage crowned with golden auras
Mellowed by unrest; reclined or leaning,
Engaged in measured converse unknowable,
As one They wait for what may take a life,
As one They wait for what may take a breath;
Anon a worshipper accosts an eye
That looks at him as though it always did,
And therein finds an urgent piercing cipher,
Like as a mountain divined our passion;
Or ancient pines, scarred with secret toil,
Impart their tired snow-beladen life;
Or silent bays, their skimming rippled sheen
The whisperings of steeped secluded fathoms;
And what was rush and glee and earnest striving
Near, and almost near, an artful answer
Banishes itself, and flames a love;
This hush of reverence filters down the hill,
And soon the ancient throng becomes one tone,
Profound, mature, as ample as a ripened vine,
Devotion 'sembled in an eager presence,
Each upward hastening a prayer in place.
Now ever through inwrought marble chanted,
Where, asleep for ages, eyeless to itself,
This mute procession, mounting its enigma,
Breathes its lesson 'twixt the eye and fancy;
A single lingering glance revives that day
(Even if such a day there never was
Save in the mind's embrace of stir and promise),
Those merry folk, the herds and music,
Sweat and heat and push to stand a suppliant;
The hands that cut these blocks, that mounted them,
Whate'er they knew or guessed upon is ours,
Now by this glance, now by another,
However many weeks or years apart;
A book in stone, that reads our unturned page,
A labor in silence, a peace unheard.

The Idol

Place it on marble, and call it divine.
To this would the ancients offer new wine,
By this were they silenced when Pythia spoke;
And it was the lover whom Psyche awoke,
When hands in the darkness troubled her heart
And curious light drove their ardor apart,
But drove her in pain to the steps of the god.
When seeking for wisdom, the answerers nod
Like drunkards besotted with untasted drink.
We speak of it always, and always we think
That words can persuade what no word can say,
No reasons could charm our enigmas away.
So even the prophets, agape with their joy,
Gave incense and gesture, and poems to annoy
And to coax our worshipping hearts from the crowd.
Why ask for a purchase that flatters the proud?
Why know every answer, when answers bring death?
To pant with desire's no desire for breath.
We could pray and slay herds and offer up song,
And learn every creed that was marked against wrong,
And weep at the tombs, and witness at birth,
And show to our children the lessons of mirth,
And place it on marble, and give it our praise:
No lightning as sudden as unvalued days.
We live with this worship we seek in the sky;
The idol our wishes, the marble our eye.

Sometimes the dreams I taste begin a wine
That yields up gall the moment I would drink;
Sometimes the words I pen could make me think
How leisure of the tongue is not divine;
And, as Odysseus sailed the lonely brine,
Expectant of home where the homeless sink,
So must I watch the drowsy hours wink,
These waves of fancy that are never mine.
And yet, the moment comes. Then did Plato's Lord
Ignore polemics from the learnéd horde
And stand in silence on his marble porch;
Then 'mid night eternal, men gasped shivering –
A star from shadows loomed – heat quivering
Danced about Prometheus' wily torch.

This is not heaven, what my mind adorns:
No burnished gates ope wide a rainbow sky,
No windy seraphs blare their mystic horns
Nor proffered souls their grateful avés sigh;
This is not hell, this feeling of distress:
My silent wounds are not the demon's rail;
What conscience pricks, or garners from duress
Damns not the soul, though aspirations fail.
What is it then that sets the world on fire?
And what's the world? My numbered moments feel
The time and all certainty, yet still desire
The breathless kiss that pecks at what is real.
At war with doubt, but at peace to know
What the heart accepts is what our moments show.

🦋 Voltaire's Soliloquy

Were inspiration season for a jest,
Or wider moments sport for empty vows,
The wisdom of a honeyed tongue would feed
But on the lonely world's incontinence,
The millioned lips that flap their wordy breath
As tempests do the banners of feigned glory.
Yet is it so that knowledge dies upon
Particulars, and frames respect for wonder
In a gilded placard, stamped and ciphered
For a lunatic to martial even comets
Into explanation? Who tutored air?
Who would discipline the sun to gainsay fire?
When even children titter with the wind
And fling their playful baubles at the moon,
Why must we – who shroud our phantom conscience
In a pampered bosom, only to have it
Rend and gnaw our inmost assignations,
As did his violent, lupine trophy nibble
At the Spartan youth's impassive prudence –
Why must we return a jewel with fashion?
Why must we dangle observation forth,
A pendulum to clever infamy,
When every pearl that gains the rising tide
Of artistry comes unbidden to our speech
Yet mouths the very ocean of our soul?
Oh damn! Has vanity become a genius!
The heathen muse of perfumed eloquence
Dab its gaudy dust at modesty!
Voltaire,
You've spurred the patience of a cautious mind
Unto the very brink of definition;
You've driven needles into complacency,
Provoked the bloated smirk, unsettled truth,
Distracted learning, abandoned fantasy
And squeezed the succulent pulp of questioning
Until its bitter rind persuaded you
To drink deep the oozings of perplexity,

But leave the gall for Sophists. Have you learned?
Or are the leavings of forbidden fruit
Intended to incise where they inform?
I question not inspiration: I kneel.

Persuade yourself that friendship understands
To cull fruition from abandonment;
The summer rains have all their flowers sent
A fragrant spray to grey September's hands.
Regard it not that autumn sorrow spans
Both honeyed sun and wintery interment;
A fallow heart contains the sweet ferment
That pours its heady mirth on tired lands.
I watch the sky. The brittle leaves unpin
Themselves and swirl aloft; the teeming birds
Cavort in graceful arcs. Both purge the trees:
One, as spangled witness to our fallen
Minutes; the other, purposed, like the words
A Teacher offers when certainty flees.

Let me kiss your eyes without an embrace,
And whisper glances silent in their trust;
Discourage them, but let not words erase
This tender discourse, though your feelings must.
Who yielded ever only to a look?
Who conquered passion with a hungry eye?
Yes, often we from parted lids mistook
A friendly sparkle for an earnest sigh;
And all of love and hate is but a gleam
That fires us to caresses or disdain:
What you see now is how I want to seem,
What I see is what I would have remain,
But oh! you blink, as though to bid adieu!
Release me, then; yet I will still hold you.

There was a time when poets inked the soul
Of one they loved or pined for in sweet gloom;
Back then their lines, like roses in a bowl,
Lay deftly placed and swelled a grand perfume;
They called on winds and stars and gods at play
To parallel the fires in their breast,
And either cursed the darkness or the day,
Which kept them where their yearnings had no rest.
But you, my love, are not a painted phrase,
You are what seeks to issue from my quill;
When I of you descant in measured lays
Such hints of beauty guard your beauty still,
For here's the puzzle, sets all praise to flight:
You are not "like" – you are what I would write.

Your love is not my love. Who does not say,
Why would you love me? This belovéd one,
Who could he be? My inward mirror may
Suggest a pleasing form, but fancies run
Against what they would see, and see what is.
To behold what is beheld stops all sight –
Our measure of our deeds but perishes,
And doting on one's worth is meager light.
My light is loving what you ever are,
The quiet waters of a spring eterne,
Reflected there, the reverence of a star,
Whose glowings for another softly burn;
So love you what I love, and this pursue,
That loving what is me, is loving you.

To Denmark

Land of silent dreaming! Where naked day
And frozen night are both eternity!
Elsinore broods above the misty sea,
As when Hamlet's sire shunned the morning ray.
Emerald birch trees shimmer, the cygnets play,
And through the merchants' copper-towered city
Beautiful girls have always smiled sweetly,
Even while Kierkegaard penned his fearful lay.
But most of all, Andersen's dream is yours:
Now wind and tree and duck and toy and quill
Are ever wise with Fancy's magic breath;
Still weeps that finless maid by lonely shores,
And haunting peace of the Nightingale's trill
May charm another Emperor from death.

To the Stars

I am but silent, and I drink no wine.
The evening sky pretends to fall asleep;
As nod my thoughts, so nonchalantly shine
Those distant eyes, whose dreams the angels keep.
There was a moment when I thought I knew
What meaning lies beyond their patterned gaze,
As though, to link those vital points, I drew
The huge enigma that each night displays.
Sometimes it seems so clear, yet cannot be,
For wisdom pencils not her brighter soul;
So soon the misty morning draws on me
And drops its lids on what the darkness stole.
I think of this – and pour myself a cup;
When They withdraw, then I must raise it up.

✒ The Goddess

One night a whisper roused me from my sleep
Into a dream. It was an umber dream,
And there were many clouds upon bare hills,
And waves of mist that lapped against the air,
Which either side enfenced a single road
Where I kept pace. I waited as I walked,
Aware that to decide was to pretend.
In this grey world there was not loneliness;
My breast and entrails knew a steady rhythm
Surged about all sides with life and living,
My mind kept check on every yesterday,
And I knew I was not lost, but challenged.
Again it came, a gust of hushing wind,
A whispered cry, before me and one side,
And with it came a form like twisting smoke;
It rose and rippled, darker grey on grey,
And outlines soon appeared of tunic folds,
And two arms raised together overhead
That framed a pallid mouth and cheeks and eyes,
With puffs of dusty hair surrounding it;
As we watch wreaths escape a chimneypiece,
Both visible and nothing, shaping no shape,
Thus captured I the form of a woman –
Lace of ocean foam curling into fizz,
Restless swallows in their circumscribed flock,
Flinches of worried passion in the eye,
Always changing what they always remain –
Like this the apparition kept her place,
Eternal unquiet in quiet poise.
Our words filled less than the hail of strangers,
Yet an intimate urgency stripped me.
She knew me. I knew this, not knowing her.
We vanished and appeared beside a wall.
I grew afraid, and she gave me no ease,
But knelt with still-raised arms and whispered low
This now accustomed hush, like burning ice,
"What do you want?" she said, "What do you do?"

A simple passage of immortal breath,
Like draughts of wind across a graveyard.
To say I dreamed is not to say I slept;
Sometimes we see, though dreaming, that we dream,
And thus the phantoms make a double press –
They slay our sleep, but do it in a story,
Rousing for us enchanted troubles,
While they escape. An ether kiss remains,
A burden only we can voice, and live,
And who would question our doubt of no thing?
You must allow me impossibility,
You must permit it, that a human mind
Would succumb before a pillar of mist,
Would press hot water from its bones and flesh
And find itself more empty than this air.
This dream does not continue anymore;
I fear the goddess and her honesty,
Though reading this you will not fear the same.

To a Hummingbird

We always wish for Summer to remain,
The diamond noon of gold and luscious green,
When full-grown arbors sway with sunlight rain,
And tumbling finches twitter as they preen,
Then flick, and spurt, like bubbles foam on burnished sheen
Of merry rivers; long and longer days
Confound the stars with friendly arms of blue;
I walk intoxicated here, where Phoebus plays
His harp of light and charms the seed anew,
Begging for a happy glimpse of you.

Here, where ripening liquors drown our sense
And lull us into love, the swollen bees
Carouse in swarms, drunk with pollen incense
And the lazy drift of noontide's mild breeze;
And roses toast the sun with silky cups, to please
The thickened air with new unfolding wine;
Their heady draught oozes round my lips, hung
Like perfume dew; phantom clusters on a phantom vine,
Which ferment as they blossom on the tongue
And swell the heart with music never sung.

Now appear! and, like an emerald sunbeam,
Rush to stir before the nectar's lip,
Perched on the air your anxious pinions teem,
Then quickly dart an eager needle-sip
To suck the budding sugar, while tender blooms tip
Their sweet increase and sate thy trembling thirst.
Such visions tease the soul: my eyes beguile
My mind to witness such intensity of purpose burst
In lovely fury. As a god might smile
You linger here, but flutter all the while.

What is the lesson of this busy grace?
When shall we pause like you? pause eternal
With a fervent heart quivering in space?

In gloom the dreamy owl keeps nocturnal
Watch with eyes like moons, in fear the cold, infernal
Cobra sways his head with cunning eagerness;
But our vigilance must be of finer keep,
The sweet persuasion of a Naiad's tenderness
That prods the clapping butterflies from sleep,
And sprinkles water when Her mirrors weep,

And lifts you on your way, immortal One!
So might I fly on palpitating art
And pluck a crazy virtue from the sun!
Persuade the world with plunging wings apart
To flay the strident air with music of the heart!
So might I fly!! –
                            But I am startled now.
This juice that nurtures you quickens to fire;
What dulls the one may rouse another's sleeping brow,
Apollo thrills both measures from His lyre:
A dire wisdom, or a wise desire;

For, you are gone. As goes each single day.
How quickly time will come and dally near,
Then feed on action and be sped away.
We always wish for Summer to appear,
The patient wisdom of the yet impatient year.
Tomorrow's but a hint, the moment tells,
And only of today we drink our fill;
I watch you dance away amid the nodding bells...
So go, and come, as suits your sudden will;
Beggars must wait, and I am waiting still.

Encountering Oscar Wilde's Monument in Pére Lachaise

We met each other without ceremony,
So like the time your book was handed me.
I then but had the vaguest word of "Oscar,"
And now I only knew the stone existed.
To not expect is not without its purpose,
A moment comes, it teaches, and we pass.
It was autumn, cold light and threadbare trees,
Quiet, like the visitors to these graves.
Nothing I looked for, just to walk alone,
And so I recognized it sans fillip.
There was no music there. It made me pause.
A buff white stone, your name in proper cut,
Surrounded by a horde of felt-tip "me's,"
With a gaudiness betraying transience.
Such scribbled appeals to our memory,
Were they not acquiescing that we perish?
Were they not begging for a death like yours?
A couple paused when I did. We looked around,
Four younger people came soon after.
Words were said, we looked from different angles.
This was not art, but it was not useless.
The silence of it all enthralled me:
Why do we pause? To what do we hearken?
I glanced at your name again, tried to fix it,
Walked away, and turned round several times.
Like the steady press of one organ key,
A murmur of yourself, it stays with me.

St. Thomas and Mary Magdalene

MARY

Why would I touch what is not yet my own?
Why do I want you? What is it I seek?
How often, when I wandered by your side,
Or sat with you at table in the night,
Or watched you rest upon a rock and gaze
At us with that sweet repose of spirit
Which, like a welcome hearth in winter,
Was all warmth and glow and reason to be
Together, how often were we only
Friends, companions merely: I, a servant
And a tender hand, and you, the answer,
And the pivot of a thousand wheels, and words
Like ripening vines that, when crushed by deeds,
Yielded an uncompromising liquor,
So bitter to my tremulous sip, but so
Intoxicating to my anxious blood
That I could bear a blaze within my breast
And yet was not consumed by what you showed
And what I plainly saw. How gently you
Smiled when we tried to understand, or when
I helped you wash your cloak, or even when
They beat you with their rods. You smiled in death,
Though the pain was terrible, and not abstract,
Nor desired, nor even comprehended,
No, not even this. You were dead. That was
Not possible. How could you go away?
That quiet voice, those eyes, and your white hand,
The thousand joys we all embraced with you,
The bread we took together – all was gone.
Each morning I arose and sunlight came,
And I ate and washed, and you were not here;
And I walked to the well, and children played,
And birds pecked among them, and I met my friends
And did not meet you; and I sang my song,
And drew the water – and you still were gone.
Yes, you were gone. You had become silence.

What was warmth and fullness was now a void;
And it was open, and still. And between
Myself and all I spoke – and everyone
I knew, and every tree and house and beast
I saw – between myself and all of this
There grew this ever-widening silence.
Oh, it grew so large, My Lord, so heavy;
I was big with it, it weighed close on me
So I would cry and beg travail away.
And by the silent rock I stood and watched
For you, and knew not why I watched for you.
I waited, and the world was still, and none
Could comfort me.
                     Now you are here again.
How I longed to touch you, to know that you
Were living still! How I wanted for you
To see me and invite my embrace! But
I cease this now. For I have reached for you,
And you have said, "No." To be with you
Was always hard, to respect that distance
Between your heart and ours; but to see you
As I have wished to see you, to speak with
You again as I have yearned for more than
Warmth upon my cheek, but then to feel you
So undeniable and so exact –
This is distance to sudden to embrace.
I stand on a chasm, and the silent world
Around is a friendly terror. Please
Let me take your hand. I watch my teardrops
Fall into eternity; my sorrow
Falls with them. You gaze at me so fondly,
As though uncertainty were a blessing,
Even a fulfillment. Must you leave again?
But maybe it is not this way, maybe
It is I who must return from something
Unobserved and dead. Even now, as you
Disperse before the sun like morning mist,
I touch myself in haste to know this was
No dream, and then am startled by myself:

This is no dream. How silent is my heart.

THOMAS

Every moment tells me to surrender,
Yet I look, and look again, to find release.
The wind of your fulfillment startled us
And left us too much pain to understand.
Until that time I still could bear the hours
When you were calm and answered every question,
And leaned on me in friendship or in jest,
And hinted at a word or idle gesture
That offered bounteous meaning to my heart,
But urged my prying mind to garner truth
With caution. I searched for certain answers;
And you replied with eyes, and modest step,
And severity of purpose only found
In one who bleeds while laughing. I knew not.
I knew not what you needed, knew nothing
Of this wicked world's precision in justice,
And knew not how to beg regret away
When we all discovered frailty in our hearts.
For faith was once a service to the man –
A pleasure in respect: devotion, when
We had no other feeling; and purpose,
When we had no other wish to leave our beds.
But this faith became twilight at morning.
A desert amid gold and idle kisses.
An emptiness. A death. Impossible death.
Was it true, then, that our assurance lay
In seeing you walk and eat and listen,
And our faith but knowledge of your burden?
I was possessed by reasons, enchanted
By the glib recall of your persuasions.
How freely could I tread this magic path,
And watch the teeming crowds extend their hands
And follow us along the hills and shores,
And offer us their milk and meat, and feed
Upon your solace. And why this solace?
Why this need for courage, and assuagement

That the world was air and temporal thing?
Oh, but now! Oh, my dear Lord! How cruel is
This place of no doubting! I exist not!
No face but stares as helpless as my own,
No strength but flees like feeding sparrows,
No words but wheel like angry moths that find
The candle flame too soon. Bitter is the lie,
The dream, the pretense of wisdom, the mask
And what it smiles for. If I were naked
To the sun a thousand years, I would not
Burn as I do now. What can comfort me?
What cleanses dread?
                                    But you are with us now.
How strange, that yearning often finds its need
When need surpasses yearning. I see you –
Yes – yes, I needed only this; and yet
I am ashamed. For I have reached for you,
And you have said, "Here." From the minutest
Prick at vain indifference to that last lance
Of naïve hate that broke your humbled flesh,
It was this and always this you honored.
My fingers tremble at the doors of blood,
The smiling witness of another world.
Is this the only resting place we share?
Is this what kept you calm, and unadorned,
And free? But no, I weep at useless talk!
Let me embrace and fall upon you now!
Let me not be chamber to a heart
That is not scourged and crownéd like your own.
For even as I press into your side
And feel only air and evening sun –
And only other friends return my touch –
I am rebuked enough to let you go.
And I will teach and pray and ask no one
To tell me what was silenced by my pain;
And were it my existence you should doubt,
Then I will bear the pressure of your hand
And stand a servant with an open palm.

Two Women Sitting in a Chair

To see in a chair two women sitting,
So easily sharing one private corner,
Their hips, like two eggs, just lightly touching,
The grace of a curve a passion enclosing,
The women engaged together in talk,
Or each turned around addressing a friend,
Or both nestled close to hear someone speak,
Their bodies arranged aptly and careless,
Like as their ringlets fall forward or back,
Two roses on water, close-parted lips,
Hills in the sun undulating but still,
Birds with a wing tucked under their beaks,
Earth cut and sown exhaling its warmth,
At one with itself, aside its own kind,
Awake from its root, aware of no shame,
Here in this room, as we mingle and talk,
These two women sit and share the same space.

Venus dipped her pearly dish
Into the anxious stream,
As lovers cast their secret wish
Into each other's dream
And feel those waters teem.

The goddess, when she drank her fill,
Combed out her golden hair,
And lovers keep their passion still
With smiles and glances rare
And savor sweet despair.

Then on the eager wind she soars
Immortal as the sigh
That lost itself in saying "Yours"
And closed a tender eye,
Without the need for "Why."

Would I sit and write this poem?
I'd rather sip some tea,
Or take the bus and start to roam
For friendly company.

Would I sit and write this poem?
I'd rather sip some beer,
Or clean neglect around the home,
These rooms should not be drear.

Would I sit and write this poem?
I'd rather sip some wine,
Or lean and watch the ladies pass,
The weather is so fine.

Would I sit and write this poem?
I'd rather go to bed
And let the fairies have their fill
Carousing through my head.

Would I sit and write this poem?
I'd rather be elsewhere;
But now it's done – audacious One!
You Muses aren't fair!

🪶 A Plate of Grapes

White slender hands placed it on the table,
A silver oval bearing blue clusters,
While a passage of rough and pretty hands
Folded napkins, scooted crumbs, paused silent,
Touched, strayed, fingered a glass stem, fingered words
And with the reflex of appeasement plucked
A wet berry and hurried it upwards.
Soon the plate held only vines of winter,
Raggéd thin wood displaying pulpy tears,
A little pool of water, untouched nibs,
The fruit fermenting in our easy talk;
The sweet taste had not stopped for sweet regard
To linger over that wealth of fullness,
That leap from earth to liquid dangling pause.
How inviting were those ample branches
Of labored, long-tendered finished sugar:
Wine-black skins with hints of bluish luster
Dotted with droplets as silent as fled rain,
Bulging maturity about to die
Like full, willing lips that perish kissing,
The lesson of love from soil and sun;
And brief was the triumph of this harvest,
The moment on silver, the living jewels,
The glint and quiver of undoubted joy.
Where go the simple joys? Are they
Joys because they go? To suffer after
What we were embraces but what we were;
Let the plate, the grapes, the time depart,
Nothing ever leaves that fashions who we are.
Before you now another plate, this hour,
Whose birth a life in death will yield its taste.

✒ *Chalfont St. Giles*

John Milton sat and sipped his tea.
The vapors warmed his face. When he
Heard a light step, or the hour chime,
He met the sound as though to rhyme
It with himself – he was that sound,
That pleasant word, and often found
The silence in between. She says
Hello, the kettle whistles, rays
Of sun caress his hand, a sigh,
A taste of sugar, then a dry
Cake, and more tea. She tells him news
And tears some paper. He reviews
Her words, then she reads him the note.
Its message fills him. He could float
Upon the cleverness displayed,
But wondered why the author strayed
From saying what was almost there...
Then she rises and scrapes her chair
On wood, and warmly strokes his brow
And walks away. So this is now –
His tea, his chair and sun. He knows
This, and is still. His warm heart glows
With sound and taste and kiss and word;
His mind is clear, and never heard
A thought depart his lips without
Fruition in his breast. About
Him all is dark. His eyes are dead.
Forever closed and black. Instead
Of sky, black. Instead of faces,
Black. His vision glows and traces
Music in his speech; language teems
And rings with fervor of his dreams,
And what he feels before his tea,
And what his inner eye can see:
The friend that laughs within his room,
The fires from his heart that loom,

The terror of an empty day
And thoughts that drive repose away,
The hush that claims the evening air,
The wretched tide of black despair,
The shadows that bespeak regret
And yearn for light in his sunset –
But more than all, he sits and sees.
A man is gone. His sorrows please
Us now. We read his lofty song
And slowly pace the measured wrong
Of unjust living with his sane
Persuasion. And the friends and pain
That rang inside his porous mind
Are ringing still; the verses find
Resounding chords within our hearts
And answer all our wounded parts
Without regret of circumstance.
We read, and find an inward glance
That notes the quiet urge to be:
Just close your eyes, and try to see.

Eugene Onegin

She is smiling; it makes me smile as well.
How happy she is, and how beautiful.
Her beauty rests within her, so silent,
Like a rose, whose color and sweet fragrance
Charm one into feeling that such dearness
Can exist as light and easy as down
On summer air, yet whose very softness
Can only faintly hint at past tremors
And wet, bitten hair. And dreams sometimes bite...
Yes, she is lovely. The men sit and talk
To her about themselves and candied tarts;
And they will laugh, and she will smile again
And stroke her hair, and sip her merry wine;
Yet even when they tease, and touch her wrist,
Or ask her to explain again, or kiss,
She never need unfold her wounded soul,
She easily remains a silent whole.
They see only beauty – but is that so?
How can they bear it? How can they see her
And only speak with bubbles? How can they?
Why are they not trembling? Why no despair?
Why no longing to meet those gentle eyes,
To hear her singing word, to touch that hand,
That arm? Why? Now she turns and laughs again.
She does not laugh for me. She does not smile
For me. She is not beautiful, for me.
What is love? Is it this delighted laugh?
Is it duty of a husband – money
And forty acres? Is it the flame, and all
Its pyre of words and clutching and caress?
Or is it the daily burden, or need
For solitary having, or Peter's knife,
Or Plato's word, busy days... But who cares!
I see her, and again the rushing heat,
And she nods to me hello, and rises,
And gathers up her skirt and takes his arm,
And I am naked. Where do I go now?

Who can be my friend? I stand here and talk,
And as they speak to me of croquet games,
My eyes wince at her, but my heart too pained
To be unhappy. No, even sorrow
Cannot protect me now. Oh, how hollow
Seem the sandwiches, the leer of secret lust,
Tomorrow's enterprise! How worthless all!
Now her smiles, her imploring eyes return
For me to taste a bliss I never knew.
That tender hand, that naïve open heart,
Which only served to fuel my bitterness,
To crush the rose that newly bloomed for me.
How I remember it now, remember
Every happy word, every careless brush
Against my sleeve, every timid request,
Every silent waiting by the warm hearth,
When she pretended to sit with her book
And glanced up as I walked by her, and sighed
And clutched her blouse and stared into the flames,
And her stillness was so unnoticeable,
And I was proud to be clever... A shout!
A final toast, the door opens and shuts,
The horses strain and trot, and she is gone.
Shall my yearning pour out in futile words
Until society's wheel moves me by her
Once again? How strange, to beg convention
For my solace, to let the milieu hold
My jewel and only show it on another's
Hand. Am I so weak? Was I always so?
I could hate it then – I could hate her then –
But when hate has turned to longing, when smiles
Of contempt become smiles through tears, when deeds
Of no concern are now of dire reproach,
I have no answer more. I must be still.
Truth is so hard to bear. I want it not...
Yet I did not want what was before me
Then – shall I reject what is before me

Now? This Muse of Clarity, who gives me
Straw for passion, who leaves me dangling free
Of every touch but that for which I reach,
Is now my only handmaiden. Everywhere
I see what is not me or mine. So come,
Bitter Mistress! Let me press thee tightly
To my breast; and as I wander naked
Through this world, please but walk demure with me,
Neglecting never to mock my proud heart,
And showing me ever where true beauty lies,
The silent rose that blooms through parted eyes.

❧ *Narcissus*

If, when a breeze hissed a million laments
Among the willow leaning beside me,
Lime-yellow tears speckle your swaying smile,
While shadows soak the air and I grow chill;
At once the surface would wink with waterflies,
Your outline gain and lose amid their play,
Little teasing circles, spreading, dying,
Miming in water what I would never weep;
Now, if a selfish cloud, cuddling our sun,
Wandered between us on this limpid film –
A glint alone escapes his billowed arms –
His shade arouses visions wet and strange
Beneath the upward ardor of your gaze;
Things that dart, wriggle, ooze, awkwardly nose,
Seductive weeds, quiet beckoning tubes,
Puffs of mud, rocks that crawl, mouths eating mouths,
Beautiful horrid chaos through this wavering mask;
Is this what you hide, you who so loves me,
(Is this a mask? Is this only a mask?),
Who is patient with my patience, smiles my smile,
Who, whenever I see, is what I see?
I would soon remember eons of blue,
Your darling outline crisp against the sky,
Your lovely self so poised toward my eye
As though you'd lunge and smash in raindrop shards
This wall of light between our worlds. I watched,
I would lean and would, with your leaning, swoon;
I ached in stillness, while you were so calm;
You tarried, you never begged, or hated,
Or challenged me with what I did not know.
But now the waters move; the winds, not pleased,
Upbraid you, and spread you in wet embers,
Dispersing your still unselfish search for me.
Why would I be so beloved? I only
Wished to drink, and lave my face and locks,
And you appeared, surrendered. But were you?
Or is this, your shimmering death, more honest?

If I was not loved, if you were a phantom,
If the waves and bugs and fish and swallows,
The cold air, the ground, this willow sharing
Pity in the pool with her own twin,
If all of these remain as I arise,
(My knee joints ache, the sunlight smarts my eyes),
And only my love for you, and you, are gone,
And if, with a turn away from your grave
(Perhaps I hear the cawing of a gull),
I remount this hill down which I had stumbled,
My heart prepared to love what is not you,
It may well be that you are him they greet,
That I have drowned in air, and you, unbound,
Aloft depart to love the one you need.

Twilight

Something there is I am brought so close to,
When at this pause of daily light breathed out
And stars and shadows not as yet inhaled;
And wherever I have been it too was there,
As though a friend would pass the day with me
Without a word to any word of mine,
And sometimes wander off, or nestle close,
Or bring me water that I would not drink
But pour a stream upon the bending air
And watch the storm it made become a breath;
There are two worlds that mingle in this light,
This light! – as supple as chrysalis wing,
Or orange autumn leaves moist with young death,
Or woman's hair at rest because of tears;
And, as a candle would illumine stained glass,
With soft colors deliciously lifted
And radiance enough to not find men,
So becomes each single thing a lantern,
Throwing no shadow save its whispered soul
And easing out of brightness with no fear.
Wherever I have been it was like this:
The blue elastic light that seeps in quiet
Through the Danish air and makes all reverence;
The desert shrubs and rocks aglow like gems;
The mountain amber snows with tonic breath
And gray-blue shadows cast by upright pines,
Where crows in toil cleave as though submerged;
The mellow attitude of London dusk
With streetlamps dim as the bricks' pink luster;
The thoughtful loiter of Parisian crowds,
The birds at rest on statues or on wires
With their snippets of occasional jargon;
The mirror left by dying winds on water;
The gusts on hills and grasses now relaxed,
All breezes fleeing for the warm horizon;
And when the meditative azure sky
Is splashing out a final rainbow wink,

The greens and purples washed almost unseen,
Its parting kiss of golden ether light
Reminds the stones and sparrows of each other,
As we, familiar with another's warmth,
Amid their hair and heartbeat know ourselves;
And this farewell, and hail to farther suns,
Where death and life of nature meet once more,
Where two worlds join as sorrow understood,
And where we taste the twilight in our hearts,
Is where something so close remains by passing,
Like desperate joys suspire in success.

🐦 A Riddle

Versification after Lewis Carroll

He thought he saw a Teddy Bear
Learning to say Mass;
He looked again and found another
Birthday came to pass;
"They're easy to discern," he said,
"Just look into the glass."

He thought he saw a Hooded Hawk
Decant a Bordeaux bottle;
He looked again and found a Friend
Discussing Aristotle;
"I always will recall," he said,
"The moment I forgot all."

He thought he saw a Dinosaur
Conduct a Marching Band;
He looked again and found his body
Had become quite tanned;
"The secret to success," he said,
"Is knowing where you stand."

He thought he saw ten thousand Squirrels
Shelter a tree top;
He looked again and found the Stars
Were trembling to drop;
"Fill me another cup," he said,
"This thing might never stop."

www.ingramcontent.com/pod-product-compliance
Lightning Source LLC
Chambersburg PA
CBHW060202070426

* 9 7 8 0 9 6 5 3 4 1 5 0 9 *